CoolJournals.net

67694692R00058

Made in the USA
San Bernardino, CA
25 January 2018